The New Discipleship Guide

"Follow Me and I Will Make You Fishers of Men."

Denise J. Singleton

TRILOGY CHRISTIAN PUBLISHERS
Tustin, CA

Trilogy Christian Publishers
A Wholly Owned Subsidiary of Trinity Broadcasting Network
2442 Michelle Drive
Tustin, CA 92780

The New Discipleship Guide

Copyright © 2025 by Denise J. Singleton
All Scripture quotations, unless otherwise noted, are taken from The Holy Bible, King James Version. Cambridge Edition: 1769.
All rights reserved, including the right to reproduce this book or portions thereof in any form whatsoever.

For information, address Trilogy Christian Publishing
Rights Department, 2442 Michelle Drive, Tustin, CA 92780.
Trilogy Christian Publishing/ TBN and colophon are trademarks of Trinity Broadcasting Network.
For information about special discounts for bulk purchases, please contact Trilogy Christian Publishing.

Trilogy Disclaimer: The views and content expressed in this book are those of the author and may not necessarily reflect the views and doctrine of Trilogy Christian Publishing or the Trinity Broadcasting Network.

10 9 8 7 6 5 4 3 2 1
Library of Congress Cataloging-in-Publication Data is available.
ISBN 979-8-89597-184-0
ISBN 979-8-89597-185-7(ebook)

Introduction

A disciple is a student, a learner, and a follower of one who applies what he has learned. The main purpose of *The New Discipleship Guide* is to establish Christians in their faith so they can fulfill the "Great Commission," which is to go and make disciples. "Go ye therefore, and teach all nations, baptizing them in the name of the Father, and of the Son, and of the Holy Ghost: Teaching them to observe all things whatsoever I have commanded you; and, lo, I am with you always, even unto the end of the world" (Matthew 28:19–20).[1]

This guide is a teaching tool for new believers in Christ, and also for anyone curious and seeking to learn about Christianity or for someone seasoned in the faith who can use it for Bible study, as it is power packed with the Word of God. This material is designed to develop individuals to become more like the Savior. Jesus became man, lived on earth, and experienced the trials and persecutions that man suffers in order to prove Himself as a perfect example for us. These lessons show the character of Christ. "For even hereunto were ye called because Christ suffered for us, leaving us an example, that ye should follow his steps" (1 Peter 2:21).

As you take this course, you will grow in your knowledge of God. During Christ's three-year public ministry on earth, He called and taught His disciples so that when He completed His mission, they would carry on His work. He did not leave them powerless: "But ye shall receive power, after that the Holy Ghost is come upon you: and ye shall be witnesses unto me both in Jerusalem and in all Judea, and in Samaria, and unto the uttermost part of the earth" (Acts 1:8). He gave them power to be effective witnesses.

Now, we are His disciples, and He has commissioned us to "Go ye therefore and teach all nations" (Matthew 28:19). Discipleship training is imperative in fulfilling the mission of Jesus Christ. We are to: "Study to shew thyself approved unto God, a workman that needeth not to be ashamed, rightly dividing the word of truth" (2 Timothy 2:15). This is a high-level overview of Christian discipleship, focused on what the Bible says about living the life of a disciple and equipping the believer to go to their families, friends, and communities and make disciples.

We are living in unprecedented, perilous times. People are fearful and looking for help. Thank God there is an answer for the world's problems: "Jesus saith unto him, I am the way, the truth, and the life: no man cometh unto the Father, but by me" (John 14:6). What a great time to share the good news of Jesus Christ that gives people hope. These lessons will strategically walk you through the discipleship process so that you will be able to disciple new Christians.

Contents

Introduction iii

Chapter 1. What It Means to Follow Jesus 1

Chapter 2. Jesus Is Lord 4

Chapter 3. The Importance of Fellowship 7

Chapter 4. The Believer's Position In Christ 10

Chapter 5. Forgiveneness 14

Chapter 6. The Holy Spirit 17

Chapter 7. The Word of God 20

Chapter 8. Prayer 23

Chapter 9. Fruit In the Believer's Life 26

Chapter 10. A Christian Attitude 29

Chapter 11. Understanding Spiritual Warfare 32

Chapter 12. Spirit, Soul, and Body 35

Chapter 13. Understanding the War Within 38

Chapter 14. A Spirit of Dominance 41

Chapter 15. The Powerful Word 44

Chapter 16. Changed to Obedience 47

Chapter 17. Discipleship 50

CHAPTER 1

What It Means to Follow Jesus

Many people aspire to be like someone in the entertainment, sports, or pop culture world, or like their family and friends. We've even heard people say "she or he is my idol." God states, "Thou shalt not have no other gods before me" (Exodus 20:3). It's okay to admire those who are talented and have great skills, but remember, you are special in the eyes of God, created in His image and likeness, and He has given you a unique talent and gift.

We follow Christ because He is the believer's ultimate source of moral guidance that gives us not only eternal life but a deeper meaning to life. We follow Christ because He is the only one that went to the Cross of Calvary, died for our sins, rose on the third day with all power in His hand, and now is sitting on the right-hand side of God making intercession for us. Following

Christ is believing that He is who He says He is. It is then declaring Jesus is Lord and being baptized in His name that we make the first steps of obedience in following Jesus. Also, Jesus said, "If any man will come after me, let him deny himself, and take up his cross, and follow me. For whoever wishes to save his life shall lose it; but whoever loses his life for my sake shall find it" (Matthew 16:24–25). Following Jesus is to be willing to sacrifice your own comfort for the sake of serving Christ and others, apply His teachings, and obey His Word.

To be a disciple of Christ, one must be willing to come. Jesus will not force you to follow Him. Regardless of your ethnicity, social status, or gender, whoever is willing, let him come. Following Christ is a sacrifice. One must deny himself the lust of the flesh, bad attitudes, and ungodly behaviors—things contrary to the Word of God. Are you willing to lose your closest friend, alienate your family, lose your reputation if need be? Following Christ does not necessarily mean you'll experience all these things, but one should count up the cost. The believer must take up his cross and be willing to die to self and the works of the flesh in order to follow Jesus. We must surrender our will to His will. What good is it for a man to gain the whole world and lose his soul? Although the call is tough, the reward is priceless, as it is written: "If we suffer, we shall also reign with him" (2 Timothy 2:12).

Following Jesus is easy when all is well; our true commitment to Him is revealed when seemingly everything is going wrong. Jesus told His disciples: "These things I have spoken unto you, that in me ye might have peace. In the world ye shall have tribulation: but be of good cheer; I have overcome the world" (John 16:33). Despite the trials and tribulations believers face sometimes, we are not alone. Christ will not abandon us, and He'll never leave nor forsake us.

Now you are walking in a new direction. You are a child of God, you've been born again, you have a new nature and are a new creature. You're not merely turning over a new leaf; you're beginning a new life with the Lord as you have accepted Him as your Lord and Savior. "Therefore, if any man be in Christ, he is a new creature: old things are passed away; behold, all things are become new" (2 Corinthians 5:17). A spiritual change has taken place on the inside. You no longer have the old sinful Adamic nature, but now you have the nature of Christ and the desire to live a life pleasing to God living in vital union with Christ.

CHAPTER 2

Jesus Is Lord

Jesus did not come to earth to be served, but to serve and to give His life as a ransom for many; therefore, since Jesus humbled Himself in such a way, the scripture tells us: "Wherefore God also hath highly exalted him and given him a name which is above every name: That at the name of Jesus every knee should bow, of things in heaven, and things in earth, and things under the earth; and that every tongue should confess that Jesus Christ is Lord, to the glory of God the Father" (Philippians 2:9–11). Jesus is our Savior alone, the promised Messiah. Through His death, burial, and resurrection, we have been forgiven and redeemed back to a right relationship with Christ. Those of us who accept this redemptive work have our names written in the "Lamb's Book of Life," meaning we have eternal life through Jesus Christ, our Lord.

To acknowledge that Jesus is Lord means to acknowledge His position as the Son of God. After the resurrection, the disciples were met by Jesus, who had triumphed over death. "My Lord and my God!" (John 20:28), exclaimed Thomas. It was the resurrection of Christ that proved Jesus was Lord, Master over death and the grave. It gave Him claim to a position never held by another. Peter explained, saying "that God has made this Jesus, whom ye have crucified, both Lord and Christ" (Acts 2:36).

Acknowledging the Lordship of Christ is recognizing who He is and voluntarily submitting to His authority and discipline. One interesting fact is that all of the disciples called Jesus "Lord," except Judas, who betrayed Him. To recognize the Lordship of Christ means that you make Him your Lord and volunteer to be His follower. You can now take your hands off the controls of your life and allow Him to be in control. To know Him is to love Him, and to love Him is to obey Him. Now that we belong to Him, the scripture says, "What? Know ye not that your body is the temple of the Holy Ghost, which is in you, which ye have of God, and ye are not your own? For ye have been bought with a price: therefore, glorify God in your body, and in your spirit, which are God's" (1 Corinthians 6:19–20).

There are times people struggle with the appetites of the flesh: drinking, lust, bad moods, cheating, drugs, pride, anger, smoking, gossip, etc. Whatever it is, realize that Jesus came to set the captives free. Once we commit our ways to the Lord, He can deliver us from these things because they bring no glory to His name. If ever you wonder, is it okay as a Christian to do this or that? Just ask yourself, does this thing I'm desiring to do bring glory to God? The scripture says "that ye might walk worthy of the Lord, unto all pleasing, being fruitful in every good work, and increasing in the knowledge of God" (Colossians 1:10).

CHAPTER 3

The Importance of Fellowship

Once you accepted Christ as your personal Savior you became part of a family—the body of Christ, the church. "But now has God set the members every one of them in the body, as it hath pleased him" (1 Corinthians 12:18). God has given everyone a gift or talent to be used for His glory; the local church provides a context in which the members of Christ's body can minister to one another, building up each other in the faith. Our heavenly Father unites us so we can have fellowship with one another: "But if we walk in the light, as he is in the light, we have fellowship with one another" (1 John 1:7). Fellowship is important for:

- *Encouragement*: "And let us consider one another to provoke unto love and to good works: Not forsaking the assembling of ourselves together, as the manner of some is but exhorting one another: and so much the more, as ye see the day approaching" (Hebrews 10:24–25). We are a source of strength to each other, sharing the highs and lows of life and providing support, love, and prayer, which fosters spiritual growth.

- *Comfort*: We go through trials and tribulations so that when God has delivered us, we have a testimony to share that will give others hope: "The God of all comfort, who comforted us in all our tribulation, that we may be able to comfort them which are in any trouble by the comfort wherewith we ourselves are comforted of God" (2 Corinthians 1:3–4). As you can testify victoriously to how God has delivered you, you'll be able to speak with a conviction that He will do the same for them, knowing "there is no respect of persons with God" (Romans 2:11). What He has done for me, He will do for you.

- *Love*: God is love. In order to love and treat our neighbor right, we must have the love of God. "A new commandment I give unto you, that ye love one another; as I have loved you… By this shall all men know that ye are my disciples, if ye have love one to another" (John 13:34–35). Love is what the world is seeking. It is the cornerstone of true fellowship.

God did not intend for believers to live isolated lives; fellowship is important. We need friends; however, friendship should be based on the principle of spiritual fellowship in order to continue to grow spiritually. "Be not deceived: evil communications corrupt good manners" (1 Corinthians 15:33). We must guard ourselves and ask God for discernment because there are times when the devil will send people our way just to hinder our walk with God. Certainly, we do not isolate ourselves from the world or we won't be able to reach the lost for Christ. Although we're in the world, we do not conform to the ways of the world that are contrary to our Christian values. We're to be social, be a witness, show ourselves friendly, and show the love of Christ so we can draw others to Christ.

CHAPTER 4

The Believer's Position In Christ

I believe that it is imperative for the believer to understand his position in Christ Jesus. When Christ died on the Cross for us, He purchased our salvation, peace, healing, etc., and made us fit to be part of His Kingdom. He freed us from the bondage of sin and made us His children. "For God so loved the world, that he gave his only begotten Son, that whosoever believeth in him should not perish, but have everlasting life" (John 3:16).

Our position in Christ gives us these benefits:

- *Reconciled to God*: Before salvation, our sins separated us from God. "For if, when we were enemies, we were reconciled to God by the death of his Son, much more, being reconciled we shall be saved by his life" (Romans 5:10).

- *Redeemed*: buy back, pay off, or atone... "in whom we have redemption through his blood, even the forgiveness of sins" (Colossians 1:14). *Justified*: We're no longer guilty; it's as if we never sinned. Also, we have peace with God, due to reconciliation, there is no more hostility and sin blocking our relationship. "Therefore, being justified by faith, we have peace with God through our Lord Jesus Christ" (Romans 5:1).

- *Brought Near*: That at that time ye were without Christ, being aliens from the commonwealth of Israel, and strangers from the covenants of promise, having no hope, and without God in the world: but now in Christ Jesus ye who sometimes were far off are made nigh by the blood of Christ" (Ephesians 2:12–13). Before Christ came, Jews had no dealings with Gentiles. They considered Gentiles beyond God's saving power and, therefore, without hope. Gentiles resented Jewish claims. Christ revealed the total sinfulness of both Jew and Gentile and offered His salvation equally to both. Only Christ breaks down the walls of prejudice, reconciles all believers to God, and unifies us in one body.

- *Given Access*: "Seeing then that we have a great high priest, that is passed into the heavens, Jesus the Son of God, let us hold fast our profession. For we have not a high priest which cannot be touched with the feeling of our infirmities; but was in all points tempted like as we are, yet without sin. Let us therefore come boldly unto the throne of grace, that we may obtain mercy, and find grace to help in time of need" (Hebrews 4:14–16). Thank God, because of Calvary we have direct access to God through Jesus Christ. Jesus is the only mediator between God and man.

- *Free from the Penalty and Power of Sin:* Sin hath no more dominion over us; we have been set free to serve God. When God looks at the believer, He sees us through the righteousness of Christ. Your sins have been covered by the blood of Jesus. Prior to Christ, due to our Adamic nature, we were slaves to sin and comfortable in our sins. Now that we're saved and have the nature of Christ, we're no longer in bondage to sin. As believers, we still have the propensity to sin; the difference is we choose to sin, and now we are very uncomfortable because the Spirit of Christ will convict us, which will lead us to repentance. The Christian life is a process of becoming more and more like Christ. We will never be perfect while here on earth, but we're to strive towards perfection. Jesus going to the Cross and taking our place has freed us from the penalty of sin, the Holy Spirit living in us frees us from the power of sin, and when the Rapture takes place, we will be free from the presence of sin.

CHAPTER 5

Forgiveness

Although Christ has forgiven the believer and thrown his sins into the sea of forgetfulness, sometimes people have not forgiven themselves. This is why it is important to maintain your relationship with God through prayer and study of the Word. Know what God has promised and stand on that. The devil is busy seeking whom he may devour, and he will try to cause you to doubt your position in Christ. God did not have to forgive us—He chose to. Jesus came to save us from the curse of sin that we could not save ourselves from. "In whom we have redemption through his blood, the forgiveness of sins, according to the riches of his grace" (Ephesians 1:7).

Also, not only are we forgiven, but we must also forgive others that have sinned against us. "And when ye stand praying, forgive, if ye have an ought against any: that your Father also which is in heaven may forgive your trespasses. But if you do not forgive, neither will your Father, which is in heaven, forgive your trespasses" (Mark 11:25–26).

There are two types of Christians: Spiritual and Carnal

The Spiritual Christian is one who has a relationship with God through prayer and study of the Word and therefore has surrendered to God and allows the Holy Spirit to be the dominant force in his life, which allows him to be obedient to the will of God. "This I say then, walk in the Spirit, and ye shall not fulfill the lust of the flesh" (Galatians. 5:16). To walk in Spirit means to be God conscious, to abide and be aware of the presence of the Lord. It's putting God first in all your affections and seeking His will with all your heart.

The Carnal Christian has not fully surrendered to the Lord; therefore, the flesh is in control and causes disobedience to the will of God, which results in seeking to please the lust of the flesh. The flesh desires what is contrary to the Spirit, and the Spirit desires what is contrary to the flesh. They are in conflict with each other, so that you are not to do whatever you want. However, when you override the Spirit and sin, you're the first one to know it. The Holy Spirit convicts us, which should lead us to repent. "If we confess our sins, he is faithful and just to forgive us our sins, and to cleanse us from all unrighteousness" (1 John 1:9).

Until Christ returns, the devil will always be on his job, tempting the believer to walk after the flesh. It is not a sin to be tempted, but when you yield to the temptation, that's when it becomes sin. If that happens, don't stay under a heavy load of guilt and shame. Confess it before God and ask for His strength to not repeat it. Unconfessed sin can hinder you from experiencing God's presence and power in your life.

CHAPTER 6

The Holy Spirit

God is one and reveals Himself in three persons: God the Father, God the Son, and God the Holy Spirit, known as the Trinity. The Holy Spirit is the third person of the Triune Godhead. The Holy Spirit does the following:

He Regenerates: The Holy Spirit makes us a new creation, resurrecting us from being dead in sin and making us alive in Christ. "Even when we were dead in sins, hath quickened us together with Christ, by grace ye are saved" (Ephesians 2:5). He has renewed our hearts by renewing our spirits.

He Solidifies/Confirms Your Relationship: "The spirit itself beareth witness with our spirit, that we are the children of God" (Romans 8:16). This is how we know that we live in Him and He in us, by His Spirit.

He Assists in Prayer: Sometimes our hearts are too heavy for words. "Likewise, the Spirit also helpeth our infirmities: for we know not what we should pray for as we ought: but the Spirit itself maketh intercession for us with groaning which cannot be uttered" (Romans 8:26).

He Reveals to You the Truth of Scripture: To do effective Bible study, one must be in Spirit in order to understand the Word of God. "But the natural man receiveth not the things of God: for they are foolishness unto him: neither can he know them, because they are spiritually discerned" (1 Corinthians 2:14). This is why people often say, "I read the Bible, but I don't understand it." "Howbeit when he, the Spirit of truth, is come, he will guide you into all truth" (John 16:13). It is imperative to have the Spirit of God to understand the things of God.

He Gives Power to Witness: Sometimes believers struggle with witnessing. One example of a person moving from fear to boldness is Peter. At the time of Jesus' crucifixion, he went from denying Christ to just a few people, to standing before thousands boldly proclaiming the gospel after the resurrection. The difference in Peter was the power of the Holy Ghost. "But ye shall receive power, after that the Holy Ghost is come upon you: and ye shall be my witnesses unto me both in Jerusalem, and in all Judea, and in Samaria, and unto the uttermost part of the earth" (Acts 1:8).

He Transforms Your Character: God wants His character reflected in you so that you can remind people of Jesus and draw them to Him. "But the fruit of the Spirit is love, joy, peace, longsuffering, gentleness, goodness, faith, meekness, temperance: against such there is no law" (Galatians 5:22). We are God's representatives in the earth, a peculiar people. There should be a difference between the people of God and the people of the world. Believers are instructed to "let your light so shine before men, that they may see your good works, and glorify your Father which is in heaven" (Matthew 5:16). When you are saved and spirit-filled, you don't have to wear a sign: "I'm a Christian." Your countenance is of God. People can sense and feel the love of God in you. We are ambassadors for Christ in sharing the good news.

CHAPTER 7

The Word of God

The Bible is the Word of God. "In the beginning was the Word, and the Word was with God, and the Word was God.... And the Word was made flesh, and dwelt among us" (John 1:1, 14). Therefore, the Bible is referred to as the living Word. Jesus said, "The words that I speak unto you, they are spirit, and they are life" (John 6:63). Some ask, "How do you know the Bible is the Word of God?" The Bible was written by forty-plus authors who were inspired by God, written thousands of years ago, and yet we see today, Bible prophecy being fulfilled. "All scripture is given by inspiration of God, and is profitable for doctrine, for reproof, for correction, for instruction in righteousness: That the man of God may be perfect, thoroughly furnished unto all good works" (2 Timothy 3:16–17).

The Bible is the record of God's dealings with mankind. Salvation is the theme, and Jesus

Christ is the central character. The Old Testament shows the sinfulness of mankind and the need for a Savior. It predicts the coming Messiah, the Redeemer. The New Testament shows God coming into the world in the person of Jesus Christ (Messiah) and how Jesus provided salvation by His substitutionary death on the Cross and His resurrection from the dead. It also predicts His second coming and provides a picture of eternity.[2] (Collins, 65)

Just as it is necessary to eat food to live for physical strength, it is equally important to feed on God's Word for spiritual strength. "It is written, Man shall not live by bread alone, but by every word that proceedeth out of the mouth of God" (Matthew 4:4). The Bible contains the nutrients we need for a healthy soul. The more we read the Word, the more we grow. If you're a new convert to Christianity, the scripture says, "As newborn babes, desire the sincere milk of the Word, that ye may grow thereby" (1 Peter 2:2).

The benefits of feeding on God's Word: Keeps your way pure when you conform your life to it. "Wherewithal shall a young man cleanse his way? By taking heed thereto according to thy word" (Psalms 119:9). Most spiritual problems are a direct result of a failure to study and apply God's Word. "Jesus answered and said unto them, 'Ye do err, not knowing the scriptures, nor the power of God'" (Matthew 22:29). As we spend time in the Word with God, He will lead, guide, and direct us accordingly in all matters. The Word of God gives us the wisdom, knowledge, understanding, and guidance needed for all of life's challenges.

The Word of God is also the believer's weapon. "And take the helmet of salvation, and the sword of the Spirit, which is the word of God" (Ephesians 6:17). The Word of God also provides faith: "So, then faith cometh by hearing and hearing by the word of God" (Romans 10:17). Whatever you are going through, speak the powerful Word of God over that situation and God will perform His Word. "For I am the Lord: I will speak, and the word that I speak shall come to pass" (Ezekiel 12:25). All we need is faith to believe that He will do what He says.

CHAPTER 8

Prayer

Prayer is talking to God with a sincere heart. It is offering up our desires for needful things that are promised by God, with confidence that we will obtain them through Jesus Christ for God's glory and for our good. We are encouraged to pray. Jesus said, "Ask, and it shall be given you, seek, and ye shall find; knock, and it shall be opened unto you" (Matthew 7:7).

The Key to Effective Prayer:

Right Standing with God: "The effectual fervent prayer of a righteous man availeth much" (James 5:16).

Pray in Jesus' Name: "And whatsoever ye shall ask in my name, that will I do, that the Father may be glorified in the Son. If ye ask anything in my name, I will do it" (John 14:13–14). There is power in the name of Jesus.

Pray Quoting Scripture: "God is not a man, that he should lie; neither the son of man, that he should repent:

hath he said, and shall he not do it? Or hath he spoken, and shall he not make it good?" (Numbers 23:19).

Pray the Will of God: "And this is the confidence that we have in him, that, if we ask anything according to his will, he heareth us" (1 John 5:14).

Pray in Faith: "And Jesus answering saith unto them, have faith in God. For verily I say unto you, that whosoever shall say unto this mountain, be thou removed, and be thou cast into the sea; and shall not doubt in his heart but shall believe that those things which he saith shall come to pass; he shall have whatsoever he saith" (Mark 11:22–23). Faith moves God.

Pray With Thanksgiving: "Be careful, for nothing; but in everything by prayer and supplication with thanksgiving let your requests be made known unto God" (Philippians 4:6). Everyone encounters problems from time to time. Apostle Paul is saying don't worry, take your problems to God in prayer. The Holy Ghost is our Comforter. He will give us peace, patience, and confidence to wait on God until our change comes.

Pray With a Spirit of Forgiveness Towards Others: "And when ye stand praying, forgive, if ye have aught against any: that your Father also which is in heaven may forgive you your trespasses" (Mark 11:25). You can't go to God in prayer expecting your answer when you're holding unforgiveness in your heart towards others.

Pray Without Unconfessed Sins: "If I regard iniquity in my heart, the Lord will not hear me" (Psalm 66:18). The Lord wants to hear our prayers, but unconfessed sins will hinder that.

CHAPTER 9

Fruit In the Believer's Life

Jesus said, "I am the vine, ye are the branches: He that abideth in me, and I in him, the same bring forth much fruit: for without me ye can do nothing" (John 15:5). We receive nourishment and life from Christ if we remain in the vine, but if we become disconnected from the vine, we become unfruitful.

The Fruit of the Spirit: "But the fruit of the Spirit is love, joy, peace, longsuffering, gentleness, goodness, faith, meekness, temperance: against such there is no law" (Galatians 5:22–23). These fruits are the characteristics of Christ; as the believer continues to grow, the fruit of the Spirit will be evident, so others can see Christ, for we are God's representative in the earth. This does not happen overnight; it takes time to live holy, but as we continue to pray and study the Word, we become more Christlike, and the fruit of the Spirit will be prevalent in our lives. We're on a journey; we are a work in progress striving towards perfection.

The Fruit of Righteousness: This fruit has to do with the conduct of the believer; right living is a result of abiding in Jesus Christ. We must be an example of righteousness before the world and let them see the light of Christ. "Let your light so shine before men, that they may see your good works, and glorify your Father which is in heaven" (Matthew 5:16). If our conduct is anything less, we become a stumbling block to those who are lost.

The Fruit of the Word: Believers are to share Christ with others. "He that winneth souls is wise" (Proverbs 11:30). Every believer is commissioned to witness for God. He has given us the power to be effective witnesses. "But ye shall receive power, after that the Holy Ghost is come upon you: and ye shall be witnesses unto me both in Jerusalem, and in all Judea, and in Samaria, and unto the uttermost part of the earth" (Acts 1:8). God's Word is not just for information; it is for transformation. As God gives us the opportunity to share His Word, when the Word is heard, understood, and applied, transformation will take place from the inside out, and souls will be saved. That is the power of the living Word.

The Fruit of Praise: God inhabits the praises of His people. When we sincerely praise God, we show our gratitude to God for all the things He has done for us. It's good to praise God, especially when you're going through trials. "And at midnight Paul and Silas prayed and sang praises unto God: and the prisoners heard them. And suddenly there was a great earthquake, so that the foundations of the prison were shaken: and immediately all the doors were opened, and everyone's bands were loosed" (Acts 16:25–26). Praising God, especially when you are going through trials, opens the doors for miracles to happen.

The Fruit of Service: We are saved to serve. Every believer has been uniquely given a gift/talent and measure of faith to be effective workers in the Kingdom of God. "For we are his workmanship, created in Christ Jesus unto good works, which God hath before ordained that we should walk in them" (Ephesians 2:10).

CHAPTER 10

A Christian Attitude

A godly attitude tells the world how we respond to what life gives us, and as we all know, life isn't always easy. When we face hardship and discouragement, it is easy to lose sight of the big picture. We must be reminded: "God is our refuge and strength, a very present help in trouble" (Psalms 46:1). We're not alone. He said He would never leave nor forsake us. As Christians, especially during hardship, we must continue to strive to have the mind of Christ. "Let this mind be in you, which was also in Christ Jesus" (Philippians 2:5). To put things in perspective, believers should remember that suffering is the training ground for Christian maturity. Through these trials, we learn how to lean and depend on God. We also learn patience, perseverance, and resilience; we gain humility; and we learn to be more compassionate towards others. If you never had a problem, you would not know what God can do.

The believer is not exempt from trouble, but God will keep you in trouble. "Thou wilt keep him in perfect peace, whose mind is stayed on thee: because he trusteth in thee" (Isaiah 26:3). In our broken, sin-filled world, you will encounter difficult people from time to time. It's not what happens to you that matters but rather how you handle what happens to you. Often times when we're caught off guard, our first reaction is to panic, worry, or maybe even retaliate, but when you look at things from God's perspective, you won't take it personally; instead, you'll be able to look beyond the person's fault and see their need for Christ. This attitude comes from being in a relationship with God through prayer and study of the Word.

There are a range of wrong attitudes one can display when being tested: jealousy, lust, pride, selfishness, a negative attitude, and chronic complaining, just to name a few. The enemy would have us blame God or people when trouble comes. This kind of poor attitude does not please God but rather adversely affects our walk of faith. The Word of God says, "Let us lay aside every weight, and the sin which doth so easily beset us, and let us run with patience the race that is set before us, looking unto Jesus the author and finisher of our faith" (Hebrew 12:1).

"Put on therefore, as the elect of God, holy and beloved, bowels of mercies, kindness, humbleness of mind, meekness, longsuffering, forbearing one another, and forgiving one another, if any man have a quarrel against any: even as Christ forgave you, so also do ye" (Colossians 3:12). Paul offers us a strategy to help us live for God, day by day: just as we put on clothes daily, we must put on these attributes, the character of God. I found out on this Christian journey that it takes Christ in your life to love the unlovable, forgive the unforgiveable, and that with Christ you can have joy in sorrow, hope in a hopeless situation, and peace in the midst of confusion. We must let the love of God guide our lives, let the peace of God rule in our hearts, and live as Christ's ambassadors. Our attitude is what influences our actions. A godly attitude produces good results.

CHAPTER 11

Understanding Spiritual Warfare

Spiritual warfare is the war of good versus evil: its battles are fought daily between God and the devil; between the Christian Church and the world system ruled by our spiritual enemy; and within every child of God, between the Holy Spirit and the lusts of the carnal flesh. The battlefield is in our mind; no wonder Paul said, "Let this mind be in you, which was also in Christ Jesus" (Philippians 2:5).

Satan's Origin: The Scripture reveals that Satan is a real, evil being—not a fictional character dressed in a red suit with a pitchfork. He is called by many names and titles: the devil (1 Peter 5:8), the serpent (Revelation 20:2), the god of this world (2 Corinthians 4:4), and the prince of the power of the air (Ephesians 2:2), just to name a few. "He was a created angelic being named Lucifer, one of the highest and most beautiful of all of God's creatures. He was a great and magnificent angelic leader who, having free choice, became proud concerning his exalted position in the angelic realm"[3] (Collins, 100). He tried to become as God and take His glory, so God cast him out of the heavenly realm, and one third of the angels left with him, taking on the role of demons obeying their leader's evil pursuits. Satan, formerly Lucifer, became the adversary of God's purpose in the universe (Ezekial 28:11–19; Isaiah 14:12–20; Genesis 3:14–15; John 12:31; Luke 10:18).

Satan's Purpose and Role in the Earth: "The thief cometh not, but for to steal, and to kill, and to destroy, I am come that they might have life, and that they might have it more abundantly" (John 10:10). In this verse, God gives us the job description of the devil. When God created Adam and Eve, he placed them in the Garden of Eden, and they had perfect fellowship with God. This sinless time was known as the dispensation of innocence. Satan lurked about, looking for a place where he could get a foothold and break the loving relationship between God and man. He deceived Eve, causing her to doubt and disobey God. He still does the same today. He uses deception, persecution, spiritual blindness, opposition, accusation, and temptation, trying to cause the people of God to fall into the path of doubt and sin, knowing if he succeeds, our sin will separate us from God.

Satan's Defeat: Satan engineered Jesus' crucifixion and thought he had won at last. However, Jesus' sacrificial death, burial, and resurrection fulfilled the Father's plan to atone for sin and nullify Satan's plan. The Scripture declares, "For this purpose the Son of God was manifested, that he might destroy the works of the devil" (1 John 3:8). Jesus finished the work His Father gave Him to do, and the enemy can do nothing to alter the perfect plan of salvation.

Now that we're saved, the devil is warring against the very Christ that is within us. He will use whoever and whatever to try and wreak havoc in your life to cause you to doubt and turn away from God. All you have to do is "be strong in the Lord, and in the power of his might. Put on the whole armour of God, that ye may be able to stand against the wiles of the devil" (Ephesians 6:10–11). The believer does not pray for victory—we pray from a place of victory because Satan was defeated at Calvary. "Nay, in all these things we are more than conquerors through him that loved us" (Romans 8:37). Whatever you're going through, thank and praise God in advance because you already have the victory through Jesus Christ.

CHAPTER 12

Spirit, Soul, and Body

God created Adam and Eve: "And the Lord God formed man out of the dust of the ground and breathed into his nostrils the breath of life; and man became a living soul" (Genesis 2:7). "And God said, 'Let us make man in our image, after our likeness: and let them have dominion over the fish of the sea'" (Genesis 1:26.). Man is comprised of three elements: spirit, soul, and body.

(1) Our spirit makes us God conscious; this is how we communicate with God because "God is a Spirit: and they that worship him must worship him in spirit and in truth" (John 4:24).

(2) Our soul makes us self-conscious; our soul is our mind, will, and emotions, our conscious personality.

(3) Our body makes us world conscious: we have five senses: hear, taste, touch, smell, and sight. Through these senses, we're able to communicate with the world around us. We are different from the animal world; we can commune with God. Mentally, we can reason and choose. This reflects God's intellect and freedom. Morally, we were created in righteousness and perfect innocence, reflecting God's holiness. Socially, we were created for fellowship. This reflects God's triune nature and His love.

The devil became jealous and angry, and his plan was to prevent man from serving and worshipping God. He deceived Eve into disobeying God and then she encouraged Adam to do the same. God had spoken to Adam, saying, "But the tree of the knowledge of good and evil, thou shalt not eat of it: for in the day that thou eatest thereof thou shalt surely die" (Genesis 2:17). Their sin separated them from God; they became spiritually dead, and God put them out of the Garden of Eden. Although Adam and Eve were given a righteous nature, they made an evil choice to rebel against their Creator and marred the image of God within themselves and passed that damaged likeness on to all of their descendants. "Behold I was shapen in iniquity; and in sin did my mother conceive me" (Psalms 51:5). Due to the sin of Adam and Eve, mankind is born with a sinful nature, a slave to sin.

The good news is that rather than leave man in this lost state of sin and death, God had a plan. "For as by one man's disobedience many were made sinners, so by the obedience of one shall many be made righteous" (Romans 5:19). Thank God this one man was our Lord and Savior, Jesus Christ. "For God so loved the world, that he gave his only begotten Son, that whosoever believeth in him should not perish, but have everlasting life" (John 3:16). Once a person becomes born again, God has quickened/awakened his spirit to the things of God. He no longer has that old Adamic/sinful nature; sin has no more dominion over him, but now he has the nature of Christ and has become a new creature. A radical transformation has taken place wherein he now wants to live a life pleasing unto God.

CHAPTER 13

Understanding the War Within

To win the war within, we must understand the magnitude of the inner conflicts so that in despair we cry out to God for deliverance. The Christian life is a constant battle against the world, the flesh, and the devil. Apostle Paul said:

> I find a law, that, when I would do good, evil is present with me. For I delight in the law of God after the inward man: but I see another law in my members, warring against the law of my mind, and bringing me into captivity to the law of sin which is in my members. O wretched man that I am! Who shall deliver me from the body of this death? I thank God through Jesus Christ our Lord. So then with the mind I myself serve the law of God, but with the flesh the law of sin.
>
> Romans 7:21–25

Paul contrasts living by the flesh with living by the Spirit. Those who live according to the sinful nature have their minds set on what the flesh desires, but those who live in accordance with the Spirit have their minds set on what the Spirit desires. Every Christian from time-to-time deals with this battle of the flesh warring against the Spirit as we live in this fallen world of sin. Paul is saying the law of sin works through his physical body (the flesh) and manifests itself in evil deeds. We can become enslaved to sin if we're not clothed with the "whole armor of God" for this battle. This battle can only be won through Jesus Christ.

When Paul speaks of serving the law of God, he's referring to a regenerate man, the new man, which through the new birth has been created in righteousness and holiness of truth through salvation. The believer has a new nature in Christ that is daily being renewed in the Creator's image. God gives the believer new desires, a new love for Christ, and a longing to live holy and to please Him. You hate sin but still are tempted to sin. In new believers, the desires of the old nature (the flesh) sometimes win over the desires of the new nature (the Spirit) until the believer learns how to fight the spiritual warfare battle. We must consciously pray daily and choose to center our lives on God's Word to stay spiritually strong.

God has given us the job description of the devil: "The thief cometh not, but for to steal, and to kill, and to destroy" (John 10:10). Therefore, we must "be strong in the Lord, and in the power of his might. Put on the whole armor of God, that ye may be able to stand against the wiles of the devil" (Ephesians 6:10–11). Sometimes during this battle you may fall short, yielding to sin, etc., but remember we have an advocate with the Father who will forgive us if we repent.

We will never be perfect, but we're to strive towards perfection. Perfection will not come until the believers receive their glorified bodies. Until then, it is imperative to stay in fellowship with God through prayer and study of the Word, and in meeting with other believers that are like-minded. In doing so, you will "walk in the Spirit, and ye shall not fulfill the lust of the flesh" (Galatians 5:16). Remember, the devil has been defeated through the Cross of Calvary. Jesus said, "These things have I spoken unto you, that in me ye might have peace. In the world ye shall have tribulation: but be of good cheer; I have overcome the world" (John 16:33).

CHAPTER 14

A Spirit of Dominance

Once the believer is transformed by the renewing of his mind, the dominant spirit is Christ and not the flesh. Prior to salvation you were slaves to sin; born in sin with a sinful nature due to the disobedience of Adam and Eve. Now that you have accepted Christ as Savior, you have the nature of Christ. "Therefore, if any man be in Christ, he is a new creature: old things are passed away; behold, all things are become new" (2 Corinthians 5:17). Being baptized into Christ, you experience death to your old sinful nature and sin has no more dominion over you. Keep in mind, you still have the propensity to sin, and if you do, it's because you willingly choose to do so.

The critical order is Spirit, Soul, and Body. Since your human spirit makes you God conscious, and not your mind, will, emotion (soul), or body, the Holy Spirit speaks to your human spirit, which gets transmitted to your soul (mind, will, emotion: conscious personality). If your conscious personality is submissive to the Spirit, then the body will follow suit and be under the submission of the Holy Spirit. At this point your mindset desires to do the will of God, seeking to please Him. "For whom hath known the mind of the Lord, that he may instruct him? But we have the mind of Christ" (1 Corinthians 2:16). Because your spirit is dominant and submissive to the Holy Spirit, your will is under God's control—no longer are you selfishly seeking to please the flesh. Also, your emotions are not based on the state of your environment; if things don't go as planned or trouble occurs, you have tantrums and fall out of character. When God is the dominant force in your life, you may be, at first, startled when trouble comes, but as you remember your position in Christ, you will see things from God's perspective and rely on Him for support.

The soul and spirit must be divided for the dominant Spirit to be achieved. "For the Word of God is quick, and powerful, and sharper than any two-edged sword, piercing even to the dividing asunder of soul and spirit, and of the joints and marrow, and is a discerner of the thoughts and intents of the heart" (Hebrews 4:12). The Word of God is a living, life-changing force that works in us. With the incisiveness of a surgeon's knife, the power of God's Word reveals who we are and what we are not. It penetrates the core of our moral and spiritual life. It's like looking in a mirror; it discerns what is within us, both good and evil, and demands a decision of us.

When the soul is in dominance, the result is a carnal, sinful life because it suppresses the spirit. When the Word of God sets the spirit free from the soul's domination, the spirit can assume its created position in communicating with God, and the result is a Spirit-filled life. "If the Son therefore shall make you free, ye shall be free indeed" (John 8:36). Sin has a way of dominating, captivating, restraining, mastering, and dictating your actions. Only Jesus can break the power of sin in one's life and set the captive free.

CHAPTER 15

The Powerful Word

The Word is vibrant with life; it carries the power of life and the power of transformation. A Word that is active in us until our very spirit, soul, joints, and marrow are divided or parted; that is, until death. Jesus said, "It is the spirit that quickeneth; the flesh profiteth nothing: the words that I speak unto you, they are spirit and life" (John 6:63). Jesus Christ not only gives God's Word to us, He is the Word. "In the beginning was the Word, and the Word was with God, and the Word was God.... And the Word was made flesh and dwelt among us" (John 1:14). There is no other book you can read on planet Earth where the author lives on the inside of you. The Bible is the living Word and has the power to miraculously transform our lives by the power of God. That is why it is so very important to read the Word daily. It gives us spiritual strength for what is needed in our daily lives.

The finished work of Christ impacts every area that touches our lives, in the natural as well as the spiritual. The last words Jesus spoke before dying on the Cross apply just as much now as they did then. "When Jesus therefore had received vinegar, he said, it is finished: and he bowed his head and gave up the ghost" (John 19:30). This declaration means that our salvation, healing, deliverance, prosperity, victory, joy, peace, and everything else we need in life is already finished and ready for us to claim. For all those who receive this finished work that was done at Calvary, now have been redeemed by the blood of the Lamb and have been restored back to a right relationship with God through Jesus' shed blood. "But God commendeth his love toward us, in that while we were yet sinners, Christ died for us.... For if, when, we were enemies, we were reconciled to God by the death of his Son, much more, being reconciled, we shall be saved by his life" (Romans 5:8, 10). Jesus paid the price, took our place, and became the perfect sacrifice.

You become Christians through God's unmerited grace, not as the result of any effort, ability, intelligent choice, or act of service on your part. "For by grace are ye saved through faith; and not of yourselves: it is the gift of God: Not of works, lest any man should boast" (Ephesians 2:8–9). While no action or "work" you do can help obtain salvation, God's intention is that your salvation will result in acts of service. You're not saved merely for your own benefit, but you are saved to serve Christ and build up the church.

Thanks be to God he arose from the grave. "Jesus said unto her, I am the resurrection, and the life: he that believeth in me, though he were dead, yet shall he live. And whosoever liveth and believeth in me shall never die" (John 11:25–26). Jesus has power over life and death, as well as the power to forgive sins, because He is the Creator of life. Through His resurrection from the dead, we have eternal life.

CHAPTER 16

Changed to Obedience

Now that your conscious personality (soul) is operating under the Spirit of God, you have been set free to serve God and have been transformed to obedience. When the conscious personality is in control, it is hard to be obedient to the Spirit of God because your desires are to satisfy the appetites of the flesh. When your mind, will, and emotions have been transformed to maintain a dominant spirit, the body will do the same by the Holy Spirit. Therefore, you can glorify God in your life by being a living testimony to the transforming power of Jesus Christ.

"I beseech you therefore, brethren, by the mercies of God, that ye present your bodies a living sacrifice, holy acceptable unto God, which is your reasonable service. And be not conformed to this world: but be ye transformed by the renewing of your mind, that ye may prove what is that good, and acceptable, and perfect will of God" (Romans 12:1–2). God has good, pleasing, and perfect plans for His children. He wants us to be new people with renewed minds, living to honor and obey Him. Because He gave His Son to make our new life possible, we should joyfully volunteer as living sacrifices for His service. Christians are called "not to be conformed to this world" with its behavior and customs that are usually selfish, proud, stubborn, arrogant, and often corrupting. It is only when the Holy Spirit renews, reeducates, and redirects your mind that you are truly transformed.

"For ye are brought with a price: therefore, glorify God in your body, and in your spirit, which are God's" (1 Corinthians 6:20). You can glorify God in your body by living a godly life that honors God. For some people who never go to church or know of God, you're the only church they'll see. We're living epistles, read of men. The world is watching, so let the light of Christ shine through you in words, actions, and deeds. Serve others through church or community volunteer opportunities, etc. These things bring God glory by pointing to His work in your life. Also, be thankful, showing gratitude for what God has already done.

Share the gospel with others: "Go ye therefore and teach all nations" (Matthew 28:19). Our main purpose on earth is to further God's kingdom by sharing the good news with people. "As every man hath received the gift, even so minister the same one to another, as good stewards of the manifold grace of God" (1 Peter 4:1). Your hands and feet are tools of the Spirit of God. By honoring your bodies physically and spiritually, you are equipped to bless the people God places in your path.

CHAPTER 17

Discipleship

A disciple is a follower of Christ, a person who is a student and who lives by the teachings of Christ. Jesus said, "Follow me, and I will make you fishers of men" (Matthew 4:19). A disciple maker is a Christian, skillfully trained to mentor a new disciple in trusting and following Christ. Jesus was calling the disciples away from their productive trade to be productive spiritually. Every believer's priority should be winning souls for Christ. "Then he said unto his disciples, The Harvest truly is plenteous, but the labourers are few; Pray ye therefore the Lord of the harvest, that he will send forth labourers into his harvest" (Matthew 9:37–38).

There is a great opportunity for spiritual reaping. People are hurting and are troubled on every side with all sorts of problems and need help. If we practice Christ's teachings, let the light of Christ shine through us, reach one, and teach one in sharing the gospel, we will be able to draw those around us to Christ. Making disciples must be intentional; pray for God's guidance to lead you to those who are spiritually hungry; cultivate one-on-one relationships; be sensitive and listen to their concerns; explain the gospel on their level of understanding; share your testimony of what God has done for you; establish new believers in the Word, teaching them how to obey and follow Christ, and then equip them to make disciples of their family and friends.

When Jesus' ministry on earth ended, He ascended to heaven, seated on the right-hand side of the Father, making intercession for us. Prior to His ascension, He said to His disciples: "Go ye therefore, and teach all nations, baptizing them in the name of the Father, and of the Son, and of the Holy Ghost: Teaching them to observe all things whatsoever I have commanded you: and, lo, I am with you always, even unto the end of the world" (Matthew 28:19–20). Jesus left the disciples with these last words of instruction: they were under His authority; they were to make more disciples; they were to baptize and teach these new disciples to obey Him; He would be with them always. Now we are His disciples, and we are to fulfill this "Great Commission." We're to go and make disciples. It's not an option but a command to all who call Jesus "Lord."

God has equipped believers to be effective witnesses for Him. "But ye shall receive power, after that the Holy Ghost is come upon you: and ye shall be witnesses unto me both in Jerusalem, and in all Judea, and in Samaria, and unto the uttermost part of the earth" (Acts 1:8). Look at the progression here:

(1) They would receive the Holy Ghost.
(2) He would give them power, and
(3) they would witness extraordinary results in that order.

You need the power and authority of the Holy Ghost; you can't witness effectively on your own. This power would give the believer courage, boldness, confidence, insight, ability, and authority in witnessing. God's gospel has not reached its destination if someone in your family, workplace, school, or community has not heard about Jesus Christ. Let's make sure we share Christ with others. "The fruit of the righteous is a tree of life; and he that winneth souls is wise" (Proverbs 11:30).

Endnotes

1 *Holy Bible: Life Application Study Bible, KJV.* (1988) 2007. Carol Stream, Illinois: Tyndale House Publishers.

2 Collins, Steven. 2013. *Christian Discipleship: Fulfilling the Great Commission in the 21st Century.* Tsu Press.

3 Ibid., 100.

www.ingramcontent.com/pod-product-compliance
Lightning Source LLC
Chambersburg PA
CBHW072011040225
21415CB00005B/93